Freedom Through Christ

FREEDOM THROUGH CHRIST

A Memoir of Healing in the
Aftermath of Sexual Abuse

ELZA SPAEDY

TAN Books
Gastonia, North Carolina

Freedom Through Christ: A Memoir of Healing in the Aftermath of Sexual Abuse © 2020 Elza Spaedy

Unless otherwise noted, Scripture quotations are from the Revised Standard Version of the Bible— Second Catholic Edition (Ignatius Edition), copyright © 2006 National Council of the Churches of Christ in the United States of America. Used by permission. All rights reserved.

Excerpts from the English translation of the Catechism of the Catholic Church for use in the United States of America © 1994, United States Catholic Conference, Inc.—Libreria Editrice Vaticana. Used with permission.

Cover design by Caroline Kiser

Cover image by Michelle Bell

Library of Congress Control Number: 2020932826

ISBN: 978-1-5051-1684-7

Published in the United States by
TAN Books
PO Box 269
Gastonia, NC 28053
www.TANBooks.com

Printed in the United States of America

To all the millions of victims of sexual abuse throughout the world and, in a special way, to those who still find themselves paralyzed by the grips of the evil one because of this trauma

CONTENTS

FOREWORD

There is a general expectation in the public mind that when dealing with spiritual matters, especially those relating to healing, deliverance, and exorcism, the Catholic Church is the logical place to turn for help. Sadly, when I was ordained in 1992, I learned very quickly that the seminary had never prepared me for ministering to those individuals who were in need of this type of spiritual healing.

Thankfully, things have changed since then, and over the years, I have been blessed with numerous opportunities and people who have helped me assist those who come to me in need. This has been especially true within the sacrament of Reconciliation. It is often in confession that the priest comes in contact with humanity in its brokenness. When the penitent comes truly seeking forgiveness and healing, God does amazing and wonderful things.

In this book, Elza Spaedy has shared the depths of her heart. In recognizing her own brokenness and her need for healing, Elza has allowed God to penetrate the depths of her heart and soul. Because God is love, he always calls us to move in gratitude from self to others. While this has been a challenging and somewhat uncertain path for Elza, she has been obedient to God's call and willingly placed herself at his service.

Secular statistics regarding the various types of abuse present in our society are staggering. Certainly, the media likes to focus on the abuse that has occurred within churches and religious organizations, but in truth, various types of abuse are present at all levels of society. Extended family members and family friends make up a substantial number of incidents that occur. As Elza rightly points out, these instances of abuse leave the victim broken, battered, and often filled with shame and fear.

The devil, in all of his manifestations, is always looking for the cracks through which he can torment the children of men. His most common attack comes in the form of daily temptations. For those who have the aid of the Church's sacramental life, these daily attacks can be faced and conquered. For those, however, who carry unresolved wounds from trauma, they often need additional help to bring about healing and wholeness.

Scripture teaches us that the devil is the "father of lies" (Jn 8:44). In wounded hearts, he often finds it easy to suggest various lies that perpetuate the pain, the shame, and the misery. God's desire, however, is our freedom and liberation (cf. Ps 34:18; Jer 29:11). God desires to share with us his abundant life (Jn 10:10).

Each human being, created in the image and likeness of God, is beloved. God calls us into being for communion with himself. His greatest desire is that we come to him and allow him to heal us and make us whole. My hope is that Elza's story might be a catalyst for others who are in need of the healing touch of God. Her willingness to walk through her own pain and share with her readers the path of healing can be a great blessing for those who still "walk in darkness and the shadow of death" (Lk 1:79) so that they, too, might come to healing and experience new life in Christ.

My prayer for all those who read this book is that through these pages, the witness of one woman's journey might be a healing balm and a lasting blessing.

Father John Putnam
Pastor of Saint Mark Catholic Church, Huntersville, NC

PREFACE

I dedicated this very painful but much needed book to all the millions of victims of sexual abuse throughout the world and, in a special way, to those who still find themselves paralyzed by the grips of the evil one because of this trauma. I want to be your voice until you find your own through healing. Please know that I pray for each and every one of you daily!

You are God's beloved children and he loves you more than you can imagine. He desires nothing more than to be your healer and comforter. In the eleventh chapter of the Gospel of Matthew, Jesus says, "Come to me, all who labor and are heavy laden, and I will give you rest. Take my yoke upon you, and learn from me; for I am gentle and lowly in heart, and you will find rest for your souls" (11:28–29).

I don't know about you, but I was *so* tired of fighting this fight. Christ has already won the battle for me and for you. It's time for you to surrender everything to God. Please know that you are not alone. Keep your eyes on the cross to help you know and remember that our good Lord always has you in the palms of his loving hands.

INTRODUCTION

Just over two years ago and prior to my miraculous healing, if you had told me that I would be writing a book about the sexual abuse I suffered as a little girl, I would have said you were crazy. But as fate would have it, here I am, opening up about the most painful and devastating thing that's ever happened to me.

I was raped.

In the aftermath of this horrific experience, I looked for books that I thought could help. Unfortunately, all I could find then were disturbing stories from victims who had almost "gone crazy" after their trauma, never truly becoming survivors. Most of the stories I read were from people who either didn't even mention God or, worse, were bitter toward him, seeing him as the one who allowed the evil to happen. I believed in God at this point in my life, but I certainly didn't know him or his love yet. Still, he gave me the wisdom to stop reading those books. I felt they were not helping me; on the contrary, they were dragging me into an even bigger pit of despair. What I needed then was a story that would give me hope that I could be healed.

Then one day it hit me: why can't *my* story be the one that healed me?

While working on my other book, *Wisdom From the Women We Love*, it became clear to me that God was calling me to write this book about my childhood trauma. I will be forever grateful to the women who agreed to contributing a story to the wisdom book because it was while reading their very personal and sometimes painful stories and witnessing their courage that I myself gained the courage to finally tell my whole story.

It didn't happen overnight, but soon I began to write, and as I started telling my story, I could hear the Lord telling me to not hold back. It is only by his grace that I was able to delve deep into my pain. And as difficult as it was to lay bare my life and my soul, I also knew that I had to be obedient and do exactly what he was asking of me. After all, he is the one who brought me to this place of freedom. I also felt that I owe it to all those millions of victims out there to be as transparent and open as possible so this book might fulfill its purpose: to let God use me to heal others by sharing my story.

What I have painfully learned in the last few years since speaking out about my abuse is that, unfortunately, my story is far from unique. There are many people all around me who have gone through something similar. Sadly, I also know that not everyone has the same support system that I have had.

I also discovered there are many adults who have gone through this type of trauma as kids and have not yet told anyone, including their own spouses. I can't even begin to tell you how much my heart aches for those people! I pray the Lord will give them the strength and courage they need to tell their loved ones what they've been through. God never meant for us to carry these heavy crosses on our own.

We need family and friends who can be there for us. More than ever, I strongly believe that we all need our faith community precisely so we, by first being filled with God's grace, can help each other carry our crosses.

While I know that my case is one of the worst and most extreme cases of sexual abuse, I also know that sexual abuse comes in many different forms. The boy who was repeatedly touched inappropriately by a family friend; the girl who was groped by someone sitting next to her on a plane while she was sleeping; the college girl forced to get drunk by a guy she thought was her friend, only to be taken advantage of; the adult woman who has to endure all kinds of sexual harassment from her boss for fear of retaliation.

I could go on and on with different examples of abuse. And all of them need healing. The reason sexual abuse of any kind is so painful is because our bodies are a temple of the Holy Spirit, and when others treat this temple with anything less than the dignity it deserves, the resulting trauma is devastating.

My painful past, filled with memories of sexual abuse, had left me scarred with deep wounds that needed to be healed. After years of living with unbearable shame, I finally sought help from the one true healer, Our Lord Jesus Christ. I hope readers will join me as I reflect on my incredible journey so that he might bring healing to any other wounded soul who needs it.

1

A SIMPLE BEGINNING

A Pentecost of Healing

I first shared my story on Sunday, May 20, 2018, the feast of Pentecost, at my parish, Saint Mark Catholic Church in Huntersville, NC. Pentecost is the day the Church celebrates God sending the Holy Spirit upon his apostles and all the followers of Jesus. The Holy Spirit gave them and still, today, gives all of us who are believers the gifts and fruits necessary to go out and proclaim the Gospel.

Celebrating the feast of Pentecost will forever have a powerful meaning to me. That was the day the Lord in his endless mercy chose to completely free me from all of those chains that the evil one had attached to me through my childhood trauma.

Just five days before I opened up about my story, I wrote this note in adoration: "I knew I needed to stop at adoration today, and as I sat down to spend time with our Lord and grabbed the diary of Saint Faustina as I often like to do while in the chapel, this is where the Lord took me: page 179, when Jesus says to Faustina, 'My chosen one, I will give you even greater graces that you may be the witness of my infinite mercy.'"

It was as if Jesus was telling me that even though this would be difficult for me to do, the graces that would come from sharing my story would be more than worth it.

A Simple Upbringing

To get you to understand what I went through, I need to take you back to 1979. I was not yet nine years old, living in the city of Ipatinga, located in the beautiful mountainous state of Minas Gerais, in the southeastern part of Brazil. The area is known for its colonial-era towns with cobblestone streets dating back to the country's gold rush in the seventeenth century. I had seven brothers, three sisters, and two loving parents.

My dad worked hard to provide for his large family, and mom stayed home to care for us. He had a small ranch right outside of town where he raised livestock. He also, at one point, owned a few other businesses, including butcher shops throughout our town that some of my brothers helped run. Dad loved what he did for a living and would be gone most days before dawn, taking a few of the older boys to help milk the cows and butcher the livestock to sell the meat at local markets. I'm not sure all of them enjoyed helping, but nonetheless, they all obeyed, rising as early as 4:00 a.m. Looking back now, that was my dad's way of instilling hard work in my brothers. And he did a great job of it.

Dad was an amazing storyteller. I remember my friends used to say they loved coming over to our house just to listen to his stories. And he had many of them! He could recount things that happened fifty years prior like it was yesterday, and tell it as if it did happen yesterday. As a child, that always fascinated me.

The last few times I have gone home to Brazil, I've realized how much I miss that from him. Dad is now ninety-two years old and suffers from dementia. Sadly, he can no longer hold a meaningful conversation with anyone. I hate this disease and what it has done to his mind. Still, he has been married to my mother for over sixty years now, and you can tell he loves her dearly despite his fading mind.

Speaking of Mom, she is a very gentle woman, one born to be a wife and a mother. She possessed a great deal of joy while fulfilling her vocation with love. She used to say that even on her worst day of being a wife and mother of eleven, she wouldn't trade her life with any other woman.

I had the pleasure of spending a month in the summer of 2018 in Brazil with my two daughters while my son stayed behind with my husband. As I got to spend this much needed quality time with my mom and dad, I got to watch Mom patiently take care of her husband, who now needs almost constant care. That was truly one of those priceless life lessons. I have learned so much from my mom and have a true admiration for her, as well as a stronger appreciation now that I am a mother myself. My parents had all eleven of us in a fifteen-year span; that alone blows my mind! They made endless sacrifices to care for and raise such a large family.

Growing up, I remember hearing people ask my mom why she and my dad had so many kids. She would answer them with a question: "And which of the eleven do you think I should have said no to?" My dad, on the other hand, would answer that same question in a very sarcastic way, joking that they didn't own a TV and had nothing else to do but make babies. I did have friends who came from large families but none as large as ours.

We lived simply but never went without the necessities. We always had plenty of good food given that my mom was a great cook and baker. Hand-me-downs were just a way of life in our family. I was the youngest of the four girls and felt that I got the short end of the stick in this department. I remember when I got my first paying job at fifteen, telling my mom that I couldn't wait to buy my own clothes. She would laugh and say, "There are many worse things in life than hand-me-downs." And, of course, she was right, but at fifteen, this was a big deal to me.

The house I grew up in had a big outdoor covered patio in the back that held our large everyday dining table. We ate alfresco way before it was cool to do that. It was an easier clean up, my mom used to say. One of my older brothers had the great idea of transforming that big table into a ping-pong table. As soon as dinner was over, the net would go on and you could hear the banter about who was going to win this time. Our friends would often come over to join us in the fun. My poor parents! I'm not sure how they were able to put up with all that noise coming from the outside patio. I remember them yelling at us to stop making so much noise, and sometimes they even said they were going to cut the net into little pieces if we didn't keep the noise level down. But deep down, I'm sure they both liked the idea that we could have so much fun with just a dining table and a net.

As you can imagine, we didn't go on many vacations. At one point in my early childhood, we did have a little place by this lake about an hour away from town that we would visit on weekends. Things were definitely much simpler, and I remember how my dad's pickup was our big family car. He would have a few of the oldest sit on the pickup bed. Being number nine, I never got to sit in the back but could see how much fun my older siblings were having back there. Many times coming back from those weekend trips, one of the kids was bound to be left behind until my dad would suddenly pull over and count the heads, discovering that we were missing one. After a few of those incidents, we all learned to just count the heads before going anywhere.

My mom was very resourceful and frugal, which I know must have been helpful with such a big family. She was also very serious about schooling me and my three sisters in all the domestic trades, and I'm glad she cared enough and took the time to do that for us. Everything I learned about cooking, cleaning, and keeping an orderly house, I learned from my mom. In her wisdom, she used to say that even if you never get married and have a family, those skills will always serve you well.

Our Faith Life

Since this book will obviously deal with the spiritual aspects of my life, it's only fitting to give you a picture of what our faith life was like.

My mom grew up in a devout Catholic family, and one of her dreams was to pass her love of Catholicism on to her children. Unfortunately, her dream was not our reality back then because my dad was not Catholic. In fact, he was not religious at all and actually had a strong disdain for the

Catholic Church. He claimed that he didn't believe in orga-
nized religion. I love my dad, but I respectfully have to say
that he was very wrong on this one, as I would eventually
discover.

When I was about eight or nine years old, our weekly
visits to Mass abruptly ended. I had always assumed it was
because my dad pressured my mom to stop going, and just
recently my suspicion was confirmed. As the head of our
household, my dad made the decision that would change all
of our lives.

Even though we stopped going to Mass, by the grace of
God, the seeds my mom had planted in me were already
rooted. I was Catholic in my heart and my soul. As I got into
my teenage years, I would sometimes go to Mass with my
friends. I remember thinking how lucky they were to have
parents that cared enough to take them to church.

Thankfully, I had lots of good examples of faithful Catholic women in all my aunts (my mom's sisters). Later, they
told me how much they prayed for us and how, just as I sus-
pected, it was very difficult and painful for my mom to have
to give up her faith. When I was a teenager, I remember my
mom telling me to marry a man who shared my faith. She
understood how important that was and wanted to spare me
the heartache and disappointment that comes from being
in a marriage without God resting at its center. Thank God
my mom had enough courage to tell me the hard truth. Yes,
she loved my dad, but she still wished they shared the same
faith.

So this was my simple upbringing. Some disappointments
but mostly happy times, probably not much different from

yours. But one horrible day, my carefree world got turned upside down.

2

THE WOUND

The Grooming Process

I mentioned our family home before. It was located on the backside of a typing school, right next to a Jehovah's Witness hall. At the time, my two older brothers attended their services, but the rest of the family did not participate. The street was filled with families with lots of kids, and everyone pretty much knew each other. My dad owned the typing school and my older brother managed the business. Since the store was attached to our home, all of us kids came and went whenever we pleased.

The man who would become my abuser was a trusted employee of the business. He was single, in his late forties, and a respected member of the Jehovah's Witness community. The fact the he attended services with members of my family, and that he was an employee, gave my parents no reason to suspect that he would harm any of us.

Since I was always in and out of the business office, it made it easy for him to start his grooming process. Every time I came in to the shop, he would say hello and offer me candy that he kept in his pocket. This grooming process happened over many months, and in my naive and juvenile mind (remember, I was not yet nine), I thought he was a friend.

The inappropriate behavior began when he would ask me to sit on his lap. This lasted for awhile until it wasn't enough for him. That's when the grooming process took a devastating turn. The touching escalated from over my clothes to under them. He would force me to touch him, but because our time alone was limited, he knew he could only go so far. While he was molesting me, he would say, "You're such a bad girl. If you ever tell anyone about this, you know they are going to say it's your fault. No one will believe you."

And I believed him.

This marked the beginning of the mental abuse and manipulation. In my long research into this subject, I have found that this mental abuse is something that almost always accompanies cases of sexual abuse (or any other type of abuse). The perpetrator will do and say just about anything to make you believe it's all your fault. That's when he, in his very sick mind, knows he has control over you and can continue with the abuse without worrying about the victim telling anybody.

I Wanted to Die

He had me now. I was powerless because I believed his lies. How could I tell my parents what was happening when I thought it was my fault?

That's when he decided to lure me to his house with the promise of a special present. He lived just a few blocks away, and back then, kids were allowed to roam free until dinnertime. I remember being so excited to see what present he had for me.

Writing this is very difficult. Every time I go back to that day, I feel physically sick to my stomach and get tears in my eyes. I cry for that little girl who had no idea what she was walking in to. I wish I could scream, "Don't go in there! Your life will never be the same!"

When I walked into his small house, he immediately locked all the doors. The disgusting sneer on his face told me something sinister was about to happen. He grabbed my hand and led me to his bedroom. That's when he began undressing me, and I completely froze.

Victims in traumatic situations do one of three things: fight, take flight, or freeze. This threefold response is a physiological reaction that occurs during a harmful event, attack, or threat to survival. My little body froze. My mind did too, for many years.

He raped me in the middle of the day, right there in his room. While my tiny body lay there, my mind went crazy. I wanted to die, and even though I was so young, I knew there was something terribly wrong and evil going on. I also knew that I would never be the same. The smell of his body would haunt me for years to come.

Walking home that day, I felt so dirty, and throughout my childhood that feeling never went away. No child should have to live with that kind of torment. I was too scared and in shock to tell my parents; I believed I would be punished for what happened. My abuser told me, "This is what happens to bad little girls," and I felt like the worst little girl on the planet.

I apologize for giving such detail, but I know that God wants me to tell my whole story. Only then can it possibly bring healing to others who have been through similar traumas.

Living with Lies

To my surprise and relief, my abuser confessed the rape to another member of the Jehovah's Witness organization. That person told my dad what happened. I remember my dad being understandably enraged. "I'm going to kill the son of a bitch!" he screamed.

Before my dad could take matters into his own hands, the elders of the organization helped my abuser leave town. Shame on them for protecting him and leaving an innocent little girl to pick up the pieces! I've never seen him again but have often wondered if he went on to molest and rape more little girls. I pray to God he didn't!

Through the trauma of sexual, physical, or mental abuse, the evil one instills in the victims all kinds of lies. In my case, those lies were:

> **First Lie:** It must have been my fault.
>
> For crying out loud, I was eight years old! How could that have been my fault?
>
> **Second Lie:** I should be forever ashamed.
>
> This one probably hurt me the most because shame is what kept me from talking about what happened and finding the help I so desperately needed.
>
> **Third Lie:** I'll never find happiness.

This lie made me believe that God didn't really love me since he allowed this to happen.

I believed in these lies so much that in my twenties, I realized I was sabotaging my own happiness by being drawn to people that would hurt me.

Yet these lies have also fueled my resolve to write this book. This book is for those victims who have been holding on to all the lies the evil one has instilled in them through the terrible trauma of abuse, in whatever form they may have experienced. Please remember that the devil's goal is to destroy all of God's children. I beg you to stop believing in these lies or any others he tries to make you believe. Whatever happened to you was not your fault! You should not be ashamed any longer!

My prayer is that by the time you're finished reading my story, you'll resolve to stop believing in the lies and look for help so you can also find your freedom through Christ like I have. Our God is a loving God who desires to heal every single one of his beloved children the same way he has healed me. I believe now that what happened to me was truly the work of the evil one. God, in his goodness, has given all of us the free will to choose, and that man chose to exercise evil.

The *Catechism of the Catholic Church* has this to say about free will and our freedom to choose: "While allowing us to make our own choices, our freedom is fulfilled and 'attains its perfection when directed towards God'" (CCC 1731). So now I have the freedom to choose to listen to what God wants from me. He wants to use my pain and suffering to heal others and to show them a path out of the darkness. He longs to be our healer and our comforter.

After my parents found out what happened, they took me to a doctor to make sure I was physically okay. But no counseling was provided for the mental and spiritual damage that had been done. After that doctor's visit, nothing was ever said to me about the abuse. Maybe they thought, because I was so young, I would just forget about what happened.

Whatever the case, I don't blame my parents and don't want to broach this with them all these years later. I don't want them to feel guilty for not knowing what to do for me back then. I now believe they thought they were doing the right thing by *not* talking about it, and I also believe they had no idea how to handle something like this. It was a different world back then and no one wanted to talk about this taboo topic. Some unfortunately still don't want to talk about it today.

I'm here to tell you from experience that keeping it in the dark hurts the victim even more. It allows Satan to toy with the victim and be a bully, pushing those lies I just highlighted. If you are the parent of a child who has gone through this type of trauma, I urge you to sit down and talk to your child. Let her know that you are there for her. And look for the right people who can best help her work through her pain, preferably someone with the understanding that Jesus is the ultimate healer.

Through God's goodness, I was able to have a somewhat normal childhood. My sister Catia told me a few years ago that she was amazed at how I was able to survive and thrive after what I went through. I told her it was God who helped me move past the pain, to not let it define me, or worse yet, destroy me. Everything comes from him. Everything is accomplished by and with his grace. And any attempt at healing in the aftermath of abuse without him is in vain.

3

FINDING HEALING THROUGH CHARITY AND FORGIVENESS

In Search of a Safe Space

In 1986, when I was barely seventeen, my dad and I visited my sister and her husband living in Boston. I fell in love with America so much that I begged my dad to let me stay. But he was uncomfortable with the idea because I was so young.

After a while, he agreed to let me stay and live with my sister and her husband. I got a part-time job and started taking English as a second language classes at night. Shortly thereafter, I started dating one of my coworkers, and soon we were married. I was eighteen and he was twenty-one. We were two kids who had no idea what we were getting in to.

As you can imagine, my parents were less than thrilled about us getting married at such a young age. Looking back, I realize I was only searching for my safe space, a place where I could feel protected. We weren't a good match for many reasons, one of them being that he never wanted to have children (something I found out *after* we were married). I felt betrayed. We divorced two years later. Thankfully, and by the grace of God, that marriage has been annulled.

Healing Through Forgiveness

After that failed relationship, I began to gravitate towards people who would hurt me. I believed I didn't deserve to be happy. That's when my childhood trauma really started to creep back in. I was a woman now, beginning to understand how the trauma had affected and changed me. No matter how much I wanted to keep those memories buried, they eventually came out whether I wanted them to or not.

I did find some peace by attending Mass at a Catholic church nearby. I felt safe there, like some of my earlier memories of going to Mass with my mom when I was a child. I would not yet understand the full power of the Mass and the Catholic faith, but a seed had been planted.

In any event, I was in a bad and dark place in my early twenties. I was crying out to God for help. And in my cry, he led me to the Holocaust. I had a thirst to understand human suffering better and found myself reading everything I could get my hands on about the terrible evils of the Holocaust. Looking back on it now, I see that God was slowly leading me on my journey to freedom through forgiveness.

Through my research of the Holocaust, I encountered stories of survivors. Forgiveness was a common theme I saw from those who were able to go on to live with a purpose and find some semblance of joy. I wanted so badly to be one of those people. I wanted to be able to forgive my abuser so I could move on to live a life of purpose. Forgiveness is a gift that *frees the forgiver*. By letting go of our pain, we are freeing ourselves from those chains that keep us from accepting all the beautiful blessings God has planned for us.

Healing Through Charity

Around this same time, I started volunteering at a women's shelter in Boston where I met battered and bruised women running from abusive relationships. I remember this one young woman in her mid-twenties who was at the shelter for just a few days. She had to keep moving with her two small children for fear that her abusive husband would find them. How sad it was that she was running from the very person who promised to love and take care of her and her children.

I identified with their pain. Being there and listening to her story, as well as the other women's stories, helped me concentrate on something other than my own painful past. These unforgettable hours spent with the women at the shelter served as my therapy. I think it helped me to be more compassionate towards people in general. You just don't know how heavy a cross another person is carrying.

It also taught me one of my life's biggest lessons: when you focus on the hurts and pain of others instead of your own, this somehow, by the grace of God, becomes your own healing balm. Charity intends to help others, but it has a remarkable healing power for the one doing the helping as well. I discovered this firsthand.

Healing Through Personal Forgiveness

I want to return to the power of forgiveness again, but this time it's a story of personal forgiveness, from someone I knew well, rather than those Holocaust survivors.

Just after I started volunteering at that Boston women's shelter, my mom called from Brazil to tell me that my cousin, her husband, and their five-year-old son had been hit and killed by a drunk driver while walking home one evening. An entire family wiped out in one awful instant. I was close with my cousins and was devastated. I struggled to understand why God would allow such terrible things to happen to good people.

After hanging up with my mom, I called my aunt, who had lost her family. After lots of tears, I asked her how she felt about the man who was responsible for killing those she loved most. Her response was so immediate and shocking that I had to ask her a second time, but she gave the same answer: "I have forgiven him already. My Catholic faith demands it."

I had never heard anyone put it that way before. Immediately, two things came to my mind: (1) How I wished I could have that kind of faith and (2) if my aunt could forgive the man who just devastated her family, there must be a way for me to forgive the man who did those terrible things to me when I was a little girl.

Romans 8:28 says, "We know that in everything God works for good with those who love him, who are called according to his purpose."

Looking back now and knowing how good God is and just how much he loves each and every one of us, I realize that was his way of using a painful situation for the good of someone else. And that someone else was me, the very broken me. That is the mystery of divine mercy.

As one of my favorite Christian writers, C. S. Lewis, points out, "Pain insists upon being attended to. God whispers to us in our pleasures, speaks in our consciences, but shouts in our pains and sufferings. It's his megaphone to rouse a deaf world."[1]

I couldn't agree more. God was definitely shouting at me at this point in my life. In his goodness, he had spoken to me about the need to forgive first through those Holocaust survivors and then through my very holy aunt.

You should ask yourself: In what ways is God trying to guide you toward forgiveness? Is your heart open to forgiveness yet?

The answer to that may be no. You may feel you are letting your attacker or abuser off the hook. But it's just the opposite; *you're letting yourself off the hook*. Forgiveness frees us, while resentment imprisons us.

From Victim to Survivor

I'm sure you've heard that there's no healing without forgiveness, and I am living proof of that. "If we really want to love, we must learn how to forgive," says St. Teresa of Calcutta.

What is forgiveness if not divine mercy? We mirror God's mercy to us when we bestow mercy on those who have hurt us. From that day on (when I spoke to my aunt), I made a conscious decision to forgive my abuser. In doing

---

[1] C. S. Lewis, *The Problem of Pain*.

so, I transitioned from a victim to a survivor. This was a gradual, everyday process of making the choice to forgive. And as I did, I began to experience more peace, and most importantly, I was ready to grow closer to God. I trusted him more, I looked for him more, and I was curious to see what he meant when, so many times throughout my darkest nights, I heard him say to me, "If you only knew the wonderful plans I have for you."

I began to dream about God's plans for me and asked myself: What do those plans look like? Is he going to bring me a good man for a husband? Am I ever going to be truly healed from this? Is he going to bless me with children?

Soon, I would receive answers to all these questions.

4

FINDING HEALING THROUGH TRUST

Finding a Good Man

When I made that conscious decision to forgive, I was able to start trusting in God. I believed he was watching over me and would bless the faith I put in him. And one of the greatest blessings he bestowed upon me is my husband.

David grew up in Bismarck, ND, with four sisters and one brother. He had two loving parents who loved their Catholic faith. Even though we grew up thousands of miles apart, we had the same values. Prior to meeting him, I had asked God to send me a good and faithful Catholic man, someone who would love me despite my brokenness. God, in his goodness, arranged for both David and I to buy properties right next to each other.

At one point in the beginning of our friendship, David asked me if I liked to read. I said I did and he lent me a beautiful book that his mother had given him called *A Promise Is a Promise* by Wayne Dyer. It chronicles the story of a Catholic mother living in Miami and taking care of her daughter, who had been in a coma for over thirty years. The book is an amazing story of a mother's unconditional and sacrificial love. I devoured the small book and soon believed that David was going to be my husband.

Living in the very secular South Florida area, where most men were just looking for the newest thrill, I knew someone who read that kind of book and cared enough to share it with others was a special someone. The book was confirmation that God had answered my prayers in sending me a good man.

At this time, I was twenty-nine and David was thirty-one. No longer kids, we both knew what we wanted and felt there was no need to play games. I told him on one of our first dates that if he was just looking for a girlfriend, he better look elsewhere. I was looking for someone who would become my husband, someone to spend the rest of my life with, to have a family with and grow old together.

Luckily, he agreed! Our courtship was short and beautiful. Less than six weeks after we started dating, David asked if I would marry him. I knew then, and I know now, that David was handpicked by God to be my husband. He is everything I prayed to God for and so much more!

Opening Up

Just before we got engaged, I decided it was time for David to know about my painful past. I told him I had something to tell him that may make him change his mind about marrying me. I wasn't sure that I would make a good wife; I was too broken.

He held me tight and told me how sorry he was that something so terrible had happened to me. We cried together as he told me how he would never let anyone hurt me again. Something in his eyes made me believe him. And I'm glad I did. David patiently loved me through my brokenness, even in our first few years of marriage when I was still trying to sabotage my own happiness by believing those lies Satan had been telling me since childhood. Yet through my trust—first of God and then of David—I was able to gain the strength to open up and defeat those lies.

I don't know if those who are reading this have found a good spouse to settle down with after years of struggling in the aftermath of abuse. I pray most have their own David, though not all will. It is certainly not necessary to the healing process to get married.

But know this: *not everyone is a predator*. That is presumably something you already know, but it still helps to hear it. There are good men (and women) out there whom you can trust. To project onto everyone you meet the sins of your abuser will only isolate you even more. Of course, it's natural to need time before you can become intimate with someone when you have been so intimately violated, but when you feel you are ready and you believe you might have found the right person, don't cut yourself off from that person. That gives your abuser a second life in controlling you.

If you do find yourself romantically involved with someone, I encourage you to, at the right time, tell him about your abuse. If someone is going to get close to you, he deserves to know about the things that shaped you, both the good and the bad. And if he truly is the right person, if you feel God has sent this person into your life, you will get your answer based on how he responds. If he responds with warmth, understanding, and love, you will know you need to hang onto him, and he will become a great source of comfort in your healing process.

But all this can only happen if you begin to trust. Trust in God first, and he will guide you to others you can also trust.

5

FINDING HEALING THROUGH PROFESSIONAL HELP

Far from Perfect

After David and I were married, God showed his goodness and mercy again by blessing us with three beautiful children. "For I know the plans I have in mind for you," God says in Jeremiah. "Plans for your welfare and not for woe, so as to give you a future of hope" (Jer 29:11).

Obviously, things were going far better than I could've imagined. The healing I had experienced through forgiveness, charity, and trust had allowed me to be receptive to God's plan for my life and the blessings he wanted to bestow on me.

Yet that didn't mean my life was perfect. Far from it.

I began to get nightmares of the abuse. It seemed I could smell the scent of my abuser when I awoke in a cold sweat. On the outside, I think most people would say that it appeared like I had it all together, but on the inside, I was still very broken.

Aside from the nightmares, I also experienced fits of rage. Feelings of extreme anger are very common among trauma survivors.

Looking back now, I can see that those fits of rage occurred when I wasn't able to identify my triggers (the most common trigger being my abuser's scent) and do the necessary steps to stop them. I often overreacted to the slightest thing my husband would do or say. The rage was never supposed to be aimed at David, but I didn't know that yet. Thankfully, he would patiently reassure me that everything was going to be okay and that he was not going anywhere and that he loved me and would always love me.

Sometimes he would even tell me, "Stop trying to sabotage our happiness." That really struck a chord with me. My abuser had committed the heinous offense, but I was the one letting it stay with me and sabotage all the blessings God had given me.

Bouts of Depression

In 2008, when our children were still very young, we decided to move to my husband's hometown of Bismarck, ND. We felt it was important for the kids to grow up close to their grandparents if at all possible (my parents were still in Brazil). I have fond memories of living in Bismarck, especially since this is where my Catholic faith really began to blossom. We were members of a great parish, went to many events with other young Catholics, and I began to attend daily Mass quite frequently.

All those wonderful things aside, a few months after we moved, the first cold Bismarck winter hit and I had a rude awakening. Years earlier, I had been diagnosed with fibromyalgia, a disease caused by overactive nerves in the body (usually brought on by some type of trauma). The pain is worse for people living in cold climates, and the winters in Bismarck were long and cold. Coupled with the fact that I didn't know anyone except my in-laws, I felt very isolated. It was freezing outside, but inside, I felt like a spiritual desert. And that's when I began to fall into a very deep and dark depression.

The complex condition of depression has mental and physical symptoms that can interfere with your ability to function. When I think back on my depression, St. John of the Cross's "dark night of the soul" comes to mind. I believe this amazing saint was commissioned by God to go through his own terrible—and very long-lived—depression so that the Church and its people could best understand this troublesome malady. From my own experience, I can say that depression is an absolute darkness that takes hold of your soul like an endless desolation. For me, it also felt like a culmination of all those lies the evil one had planted in my soul.

God doesn't love you! You'll never find happiness! You'll never amount to anything!

I would also describe my depression as a glimpse of what hell would be like: this complete disconnection from God who alone is what our souls long for. St. Augustine said it perfectly: "Our hearts are restless until it rests in you." I can say that my heart, at that time in my life, was very restless. I was desperately trying to figure out to whom and where I belonged.

One of my many symptoms was this sadness that I just couldn't shake. I would cry for any reason or no reason at all. I felt I was losing my mind, unable to control my emotions. To compound this, I was very lethargic, always tired and with almost no motivation to get up in the morning. Thank God my precious children were small; sometimes it was purely the fact of knowing how much they needed me that got me out of bed.

Seeking Help

I hadn't dealt with my childhood trauma in a proper way, and when I found myself in the middle of this huge life change, my mind just couldn't handle it. I remember going into my doctor's office and telling her that I thought I was going crazy, that I had this sadness that I just couldn't shake. After patiently and compassionately listening to me, she hugged me and told me that I was not going crazy but was depressed. In her wisdom, this lovely doctor (who also happened to be a devout Catholic) had recognized right away what my affliction was.

I have to be honest and say that I was one of those people who didn't believe depression was a real medical condition, or at least, I thought people exaggerated it. I had to find out the hard way that depression is very real. This wonderful doctor recommended a low dosage of an antidepressant. I was reluctant at first but agreed to try it. And thank God for that, because this medicine probably saved my marriage. I don't know how much longer David would have been able to put up with the emotional rollercoaster that comes along with depression.

Soon after I started on the medication, I could feel things slowly getting better. David and I noticed a big improvement in my mood and behavior. By the grace of God and with the help of this medicine, life was getting back to normal again. I could control my emotions better, both the rage and the sadness.

I was on the medication for about one and a half years, after which my doctor and I both felt that I was a lot stronger and had a big enough support system around me that I could stop taking it.

Much of this book is about the healing I have experienced through spiritual means, but here I want to make the point that there are very real and positive means to healing through medicine and therapy. We should never seek to overcome our pain purely through "earthly" things, yet God has blessed us (especially in this modern age) with powerful tools that can combat things like depression. Of course, we cannot abuse these things and become too dependent on them—we must always be dependent on God first—but we mustn't write them off either, and we shouldn't feel guilty or ashamed for taking them.

I had to learn through my own experience that, yes, depression is real. I now have a much better understanding of this and more compassion for anyone dealing with this terrible disease that's so often still looked upon as a weakness, or even as a personality flaw. If someone has cancer, we all offer them our love and support, and rightfully so. But why don't we see the same support and compassion shown to people suffering from this deep pain in our soul that we call depression? What I have learned from having depression is that the invisible can absolutely kill you if left untreated. Do not hesitate to acknowledge your pain and seek professional help.

A final thought on my bouts of depression: I believe that one of the reasons why God allowed me to go through these feelings was so that I would later be best equipped to help a loved one dealing with dark and deep pain. I was able to recognize the signs and symptoms that had plagued me some eight years earlier and help guide my loved one towards finding the right help.

It finally made sense: God sometimes allows us to suffer so we can be prepared to help those around us who are suffering. I thank God that he has helped me see it this way!

6

FINDING HEALING THROUGH THE CHURCH

A Move Across the Country

With God's goodness, we had a wonderful new parish in Bismarck and made lots of new friends who, without knowing it, played a big part in helping me get out of that terrible dark place I found myself in. I grew in my faith tremendously in Bismarck. The Catholic community is alive and well up there, and I learned so much about my faith from all the wonderful people we came to know and love in our five years there.

My in-laws introduced us to Jerry and Sara Richter, a dynamic young couple from our parish. Sara and I became fast friends. They invited us to a gathering they had at their house each month, called simply "young adults." At these gatherings, there would be dozens of people seeking a closer relationship with their community and, of course, with God. Inspiring speakers with a great knowledge of our faith were recruited for the night (most of whom were young priests on fire with the Faith). The more I was learning about my Catholic faith, the more I was falling in love with it. My heart was slowly being converted.

Some of the wives in this group would get together at each other's homes for coffee every week. Those gatherings would last for hours, as we prayed, laughed, cried, and watched our little ones play together. They hold a special place in my heart because it was there that we became the Body of Christ for each other. In Bismarck, I learned the value and importance of surrounding yourself with good, faithful friends who will inspire and help you grow in your faith.

I was a stay-at-home mom at this time and loved every minute of it. My precious children were a constant reminder of God's goodness every day! That being said, I must admit that when they reached the ages of eight and nine, the age when my abuse took place, I had terrible anxiety about leaving them with anyone other than my husband. If they were invited to a birthday party, I made sure that either David or I would stay with them.

I'm sure the other parents thought this was strange, but I was protecting my children the best way I knew how. Sleepovers were rarely allowed when they were small. Still to this day, I have a hard time letting them go to those. Thankfully, David was patient and always understanding because he knew what I had been through. For those who have been through abuse, it's natural to be more protective of your children than even normal parents are, but we have to fight this inclination as much as we are able. We have to let them live their lives and not assume darkness lurks around every corner.

In any event, in 2013, we decided to move our family to Huntersville, NC, all the way across the country to a small but growing community outside Charlotte. Even though we had an amazing parish and had made some wonderful friends in Bismarck, David and I felt it was best to find a more suitable climate for our family. With my constant bouts of fibromyalgia that kept me bedridden many winter days, and our oldest daughter having pneumonia twice one winter, we felt we needed to make the change. Our hearts were heavy to leave David's parents, our amazing parish community, and all the wonderful friends we had made in the five years we lived there, but we had to trust that God would take care of us and bring us to another thriving Catholic community. Without surprise, he did just that.

Just before moving from Bismarck, we had dinner with one of our priests. We mentioned how everyone kept telling us there were no Catholics in the South and that we would be the minority. His response was, "Be not afraid, the Catholics down there are on fire. They have to be just to be able to defend their faith among the hundreds of non-denominations that are so prevalent in that part of the country." Boy was Father ever so right on this one!

What we found at our new parish at St. Mark is something out of a dream for any Catholic who's striving to learn and grow in their faith. We are blessed with wonderful priests, one of whom wrote the foreword for this book, Fr. John Putnam, as well as great deacons and staff. I have been amazed and in awe of the many different ways they challenge us to grow in faith, hope, and love.

God's Instrument

Even after all of God's blessings and all he had done to bring me out of the darkness, I discovered he had even more healing in store for me. Just before Lent of 2017, I felt the Lord telling me to open up about the abuse. Outside of family and a few friends, no one knew what had happened to me.

I decided to reveal the abuse to Fr. Putnam in the confessional (not that what had happened had been a sin on my part, but because this was where I felt comfortable opening up). After compassionately listening to my story, he invited me to begin an amazing journey of healing across several weeks that would change my life forever.

How perfect that it was during Lent—a time of penance, fasting, and even suffering—that God had chosen for me to take this painful walk. On my hardest days, I tried to focus on what Jesus had gone through for me, and that made my pain seem bearable. Fr. Putnam walked me through one of the most painful healing experiences I have ever had, using a method similar to what is found in the book *Unbound* by Neal Lozano. In this method, you're shown how to find and close those doors that may have been opened to evil influences. In my case, that door was my childhood trauma and, consequently, Satan's underhanded strategies. The process included specific prayers for each day and writing a letter to God about each year of my life, with special attention placed on the year when the abuse took place, going deep into the emotions associated with feeling like God had abandoned me. Had I known how difficult that process was going to be, I probably would have declined. But once again, our Lord, with his abundant mercies, and our Blessed Mother carried me through those excruciating days to bring me to where I am today.

The healing process culminated with a nine-day novena to Mary, Undoer of Knots, along with Fr. Putnam and Fr. Paul McNulty praying over me with heavy deliverance prayers, and finally, with the burning of the letter I had written to God. It's worth noting that it was while writing this letter to God that he made it clear that he was indeed there and suffered with me when I was being molested.

The pain of going back "there" was too much, and I found it difficult to breathe sometimes. Throughout this whole process, my husband was my rock, offering his unending and unconditional love. Some days he would make sure the kids were cared for while I went to pray in adoration, or when I took long drives just to clear my head. He was by my side when I was being prayed over and cried out to God along with me for a special healing.

I remember when I was being prayed over, I begged God between tears to please deliver me from all of this evil I had been holding on to for so long. And in my prayers, I promised God that if he healed me, I would devote the rest of my life to helping other victims in any way he sought fit.

It was all worth it, because something miraculous happened after going through this process. Do you remember those nightmares I used to have about the abuse? And how I could still smell my abuser's scent? Gone. All of it!

By the grace of God, I was finally set free, and to this day, I can sleep through the night without reliving my painful past. Amazing! It had been almost forty years, yet God, in his goodness, had used his holy priests as his instruments to heal me. I was free from the mental and spiritual bondage that Satan had held me in for so long. It was as if I had lived in a prison and now was free to walk outside and breathe fresh air again after four decades of being stuck inside. My soul never felt so good and so very grateful to God. I felt like I had been washed clean and was a new person, someone who would do anything the Lord asked.

All of us, especially those who carry deep scars and wounds, must realize that the Church is here to heal us. Pope Francis once called the Church a "field hospital after battle." What a wonderful image. Through the ministers of the Church, who gave me the sacraments, prayed over me, and delivered me guidance, I was able to put so many dark memories to rest.

If you feel alone and vulnerable, *there is no better place to turn than Holy Mother Church*. There you will find brothers and sisters who want to help you, as well as supernatural graces that can heal any wound that evil has inflicted upon you. I can attest firsthand to the healing power of the Catholic Church, and I thank my simple but saintly parish priest who administered to me in a time of great darkness.

Daily Mass

To close out this chapter, I want to comment briefly on one of the most beautiful gifts of the Catholic Church: daily Mass.

As I said earlier, I first began attending daily Mass while we lived in Bismarck, and it took my faith life to a whole different level. It's through receiving the Eucharist at daily Mass that I feel the stress of my life fade away.

Remember in the Our Father we pray, "Give us this day our daily bread." Jesus is telling us right there in plain language that we need to receive him in the Eucharist as many times as possible so that our hearts are watchful, so that we'll be able to resist the temptations from the evil one, and so that we may learn how to forgive.

I have come to realize that for me, receiving him on Sundays is just not enough. I'm too much of a sinner and in need of his divine mercy! Thank God for daily Mass and for all our holy priests who make it possible for us to receive our Lord every day if we wish to do so.

One might ask, why go to daily Mass? An analogy I like to consider in answering this takes me back to my childhood. Remember, I was one of eleven children, so there wasn't a lot of alone time with Mom or Dad. But when I did get that alone time, I cherished it. Going to daily Mass is much like that. I feel like I am getting alone time with Jesus. Obviously, he is there each Sunday, but those Masses tend to be more crowded. There is an intimacy with daily Mass that you don't get on Sundays, and the spiritual nourishment we can receive from that is impossible to measure.

So within the arms of Holy Mother Church, you can receive all sorts of help and grace. These are the ways I received the most powerful means of healing. I pray you, too, can be embraced by these arms and find the healing you need and deserve.

7

FINDING HEALING THROUGH SHARING MY STORY

Answering God's Call

After opening up about my abuse to my priest and receiving healing through his prayers and the sacraments of the Church, I heard God tell me early one morning, "Now that you are healed, I want to use you and your story to heal others." I was being called to be a witness of his goodness.

Jesus's fountain of mercy is endless. He wants to be our healer and our comforter. He's just waiting for his children to come to him so he can shower all of us with his healing power and graces. He said to St. Faustina, as she writes in her diary, "Behold, the treasures of grace flow upon souls, but not all souls know how to take advantage of my generosity" (*Diary* 1687). Thankfully, by this time in my life, I was ready to listen and take advantage of his generosity. Was I scared to do what he was asking? Of course! But he had done the impossible in my life; how could I deny him this request?

Still, as so often happens because of our human weakness, months went by as I ignored God's request. Then finally one day, I got the courage to go talk to Fr. Putnam about what I thought God was calling me to do. I remember walking towards his office hoping that he would say something like: "That's great, Elza; I'm so happy you are healed, but are you sure you want to share this?"

Instead, what I got from Fr. Putnam was exactly what I needed to hear. He was thrilled that I was healed and excited that God was going to use me to heal others, both in our parish and beyond. He asked if I knew how God wanted to use me. I told him that I thought God wanted me to speak to people about my healing to let them know that no matter what they've gone through, there's hope. Jesus Christ is our hope!

Father Putnam, in his wisdom, knew the perfect way I could be used to help others. He told me that he and a few others at the parish were putting together a special night of healing and worship to be held sometime in May, and he felt that I was the last piece of the puzzle. I was to testify about God's amazing goodness and the healing power of forgiveness at the healing service. Father believed my story would make a powerful impact, and with God's help, I thought I was ready to share.

Preparing to Share My Story

How could I possibly find the strength and courage to discuss this dark and painful secret in front of my own congregation?

Thankfully, Fr. Putnam had some ideas to help me. The first thing he did was assign me a spiritual director. Some of you have no doubt heard of spiritual directors. This is often a priest or deacon, but it doesn't have to be. It is simply a person who you meet with perhaps once a month to discuss the status of your spiritual life, both your ups and your downs. They advise you on areas where you might be struggling and provide insights in areas like spiritual warfare. A spiritual director can never replace the sacraments, Mass, Adoration, prayer, or other necessary elements of the Church, but it is a wonderful way to order your spiritual life and become holier.

Pope Benedict noted, "Spiritual direction is recommended not only to those who wish to follow the Lord up close, but to every Christian who wishes to live responsibly his baptism, that is, the new life in Christ."[2]

Fr. Putnam recommended a wonderful member of our parish named Jean Whelan to be my spiritual director. She was a faithful and prayerful woman in our parish, someone that I've always admired and have come to love. In fact, when we first met after a daily Mass, my husband predicted that we were going to become close friends. Boy was he right!

Jean graciously accepted the role of my spiritual director and unselfishly gave me many hours of support. We met for coffee and would talk for hours. There were days that I was on the phone with her a lot. I shared with Jean that my worst fear was that I would fall apart and would not be able to deliver God's message of hope and healing to all present that night. She would pray with me and always reassured me that this was God's work and that he would get me through it.

---

2   Homiletic address given in St. Peter's on May 19, 2011.

At the recommendation of a few different women at our parish, I joined a wonderful women's Bible and study group called Women of Joy that Jean founded some twenty years ago. In addition to normal Bible study, Women of Joy invites each woman to share a personal story with the whole group to highlight how God has worked in their lives. Looking back now, I realize that listening to the other women's stories prepared me to share my own painful story.

It was also through Women of Joy that I did my first Marian Consecration, which is the act of entrusting one's body, soul, possessions, works, and entire life to the protection, guidance, and intercession of Our Lady. This act is nothing new, as Jesus entrusted his beloved disciple, John, to Mary while on the cross (see Jn 19:26–27).

I have always loved our Blessed Mother, but that love has blossomed even more since my consecration. On my hardest days, when I was preparing to give my testimony, I could hear her encouraging words: "My sweet daughter, I know you can do this. Think about what I went through watching my perfect son, Jesus, suffer and die such a terrible death. God, in his goodness, has made us women to be very strong and able to withstand anything. I will be right there by your side." I felt so much comfort through her maternal presence. As children, are we not always consoled best by our mothers?

In truth, much of what I've said here could've been included in the last chapter, where I detailed all the help I received through Christ's Church—my spiritual director, this beloved group of women I shared a special sisterhood with, and of course, the Virgin Mother. These are all great means of grace that the Church gives us, and can give you, as you attempt to find healing. But I have included them here because they were specific actions I took to prepare to share my story in public for the first time.

The Night Arrives

For a while, I didn't know the exact date that the healing service would take place. But then one day in mid-April, our other beloved priest, Fr. Paul McNulty, called to tell me that the date had been set. The healing service would take place on Sunday, May 20, Pentecost Sunday. I was worried at first because I was helping to host a large Mother/Daughter Brunch that morning; I wasn't sure I would have the energy to do both. Fr. Paul's response was powerful. He told me that often the best work we do for our Lord is when we are exhausted because that's precisely when we let go of our own agendas and let the Holy Spirit take over.

And that's exactly what happened. The healing service at Pentecost was amazing!

When I first got up to speak, my knees were shaking and I felt like I was going to faint. But by the grace of God and with all the people praying for me, I was able to deliver God's message of hope and healing that night. I could feel the Holy Spirit taking over and speaking through me. How perfect that God had picked the night of Pentecost to be the first time I would speak publicly about my abuse.

The feedback afterwards was something I never could have imagined. I had so many men and women thank me for having the courage to give my testimony and talk about such a difficult topic. I had many whispers in my ear that my story was their story. Or that the lies I spoke about were exactly the lies they have heard in their own heads. It broke my heart to hear from college-age women who told me my testimony should be given in college campuses where so many young women are suffering and struggling with the terrible trauma and aftermath of rape that's rampant in our college campuses. Statistics from the National Sexual Violence Resource Center state several chilling discoveries: one in five women will be sexually assaulted during their college years, and one in four girls and one in six boys will be sexually abused before they turn eighteen years old.[3] So much pain, and yet if we look to Scripture, we can feel hope. "Where sin abounds, grace abounds much more" (Rom 5:20).

The Power of Opening Up

Giving my testimony that night helped me better understand what God was asking of me. There are so many hurting from this type of trauma and in need of a voice that will give them hope. I was trying to be that voice. It wasn't about me anymore. It was about all those victims who find themselves paralyzed by the grip of the evil one. Those lies had become their prison. I knew that because I lived in that prison for way too long.

This book is an extension of that night. I was confined in sharing my story to those who came to the church on that Pentecost evening, but the power and medium of books allows me to reach more people. It allows me to reach *you*.

I want you to know that this whole process of talking and writing about my abuse, not just to family and friends,

---

[3]   https://www.nsvrc.org/

but publicly, has been very healing and liberating. While I know that not everyone who has been abused will be called to witness to others like this, I do pray that every victim of sexual abuse, or any other type of abuse for that matter, will find the courage and strength to share their story with their loved ones, their pastor, or a trusted friend. When you share your story, you'll discover the healing power of other people's compassion. And there's something to be said for finding out that you are not alone in your particular pain and that many have suffered similarly or even more than you.

The evil one loves for everything to be in the dark because he knows he can manipulate us into believing that God doesn't love us, and by doing that, he can cause great havoc in our lives. On the contrary, our Lord wants us to bring those dark parts of our hearts first to him so his love can heal us and then to others so that we can be a witness to his love.

My prayer is that by sharing my story, I can help at least one person come out from the darkness and into the light. "For all of you are children of the light, and children of the day. We are not of the night or of darkness" (1 Thes 5:5). I lived in that darkness for so long, and now there's nothing I wouldn't do to help others come out of their dark place.

8

ABUSE IN THE CHURCH

A Dire Situation

I don't think I can talk about my abuse without talking about the tragic events that we've all been following on the news concerning the Catholic Church in America and around the world. Some priests and other Church leaders have committed the terrible evil of abusing so many of our children and young people. Shame on them!

I can't help but weep for those victims and their families. This is all too close to home for me, and I find myself having a hard time wrapping my head around how this could have happened. Why was everyone so silent about this for so long? Why didn't anyone think of the victims? My heart also breaks for all the wonderful holy priests and bishops who you and I know had nothing to do with this and yet will be paying a very high price as this whole thing keeps unfolding right before our eyes.

As a simple lay person, I don't have much wisdom in how to solve such a dire situation in the life of the Church. Truly, I can do very little to help, but certain thoughts have come to me in prayer.

Turn to Jesus

In a passage from John chapter 6, we read about Jesus's Bread of Life discourse. Following his proclamation that his flesh is the Bread of Life, the disciples were all shocked. How could Jesus give them his flesh to eat? As Catholics, we believe that the Holy Eucharist is his body being given up for us rather than just some symbol. We believe the Eucharist is the food for our soul. But as we read in the Bible, many of Jesus's disciples couldn't believe what he was telling them, and they walked away.

In verse 67 of that chapter, Jesus goes on to ask his disciples if they, too, wanted to leave him. Peter's response is what my response is to Jesus as I read and watch about the abuse in the Church. "Master to whom shall we go? You have the words of eternal life."

Just like those disciples, we now find ourselves at a crossroad, asking, "How can we accept this? How do we accept so much deception from people who should have known better?" We may be tempted to turn to lots of different so-called "answers" that seem to make more sense, or at least be quicker and more approachable solutions.

But turning to Jesus and putting him at the center of our lives and at the center of our Church is the only way we will make it through this mess. That may seem overly simplistic, but it is the reality of the situation.

Fight for Your Family

Though all the predators in these crimes deserve much of the blame and deserve to be punished, we know the origin of this widespread attack is the devil. He orchestrated this over many decades, preying on human weakness.

The Church is an extension of my family, and if Satan was coming after anyone in my family, you better believe I would fight like crazy. And that's exactly what I believe we all should be doing for our Church right now. We all know we need to pray and we need tangible solutions to remedy the problem, but through it all, we mustn't lose that mentality that we are involved in a battle. We must approach this sad time believing that our Church and our brothers and our sisters are under attack, and we must do our part to defend them.

Pray for the Victims and the Church

Praying for all the victims of clergy sexual abuse and helping them through the very long and painful healing process is a must. We may not know them personally, but that doesn't mean we can't pray for them.

We must also pray that those who are found guilty of the abuse and of any cover-up will be brought to justice and seek repentance. We can pray and fast for the Church, hoping to bring about the cleansing and purification she needs.

I'm all in for Jesus and his Church despite all the evil done by some very bad people. St. Boniface said it beautifully: "In her voyage across the ocean of this world, the Church is like a great ship being pounded by the waves of life's different stresses. Our duty is not to abandon ship when things get hard but to keep her on her course."

Remember Jesus's words: "On this rock I will build my church, and the gates of the netherworld will not prevail against it" (Mt 16:18). I'm hanging on to those words now more than ever. The gates of hell are always trying to defeat our Lord's Church. Here we are more than two thousand years after Jesus spoke those words to Peter and the Catholic Church is still standing strong, even if gravely wounded. Many have felt they must leave the Church to perhaps join one of the over thirty thousand Protestant denominations that exist today. But this is not the answer. We cannot break away from the Church every time there is a scandal or disagreement. We place our faith in Jesus Christ, not in the flawed ministers of his Church.

Seeing My Story in the Church's

I have found it ironic that the Church would go through this sexual abuse crisis essentially over the course of my lifetime, since my life was marked so much by sexual abuse. I was not abused by anyone in the Church, but I have a very personal connection to all the victims.

Perhaps the greatest irony is that it is this precise Church, the one that housed so many abusers and those who covered for them, that brought me the healing I needed. This shows that there is still much goodness and grace in the Church and her priests and sacraments.

I see my story when I look at the Church over the last few decades. All the things that made me whole again—love, charity, forgiveness, trust, good priests—they can be found within Holy Mother Church, and within the hearts of the faithful. And I know that, like me, our wounded Church will heal one day and be even stronger in the end.

9

ANOTHER TRAUMA
THAT NEEDS HEALING

Love Is About Sacrifice

As I was going through my healing process and reading the book *Unbound*, I learned that there's another trauma that needs healing just as much as the trauma of sexual abuse, and that is the trauma of watching your family being torn apart by the devastation of divorce.

United States divorce statistics are dismal. Some out there claim that someone gets divorced every thirteen seconds. "Half of all American children will witness the breakup of a parent's marriage. Of these, close to half will also see the breakup of a parent's second marriage."[4]

Why has it come to this? Well, many reasons, chief among them, perhaps, is that we live in a selfish society that teaches and encourages married people to take the easy way out each time they encounter a rough patch.

---

[4] Frank Furstenberg, Jr., Christine Winquist Nord, James L. Peterson, and Nicolas Zill, "The Life Course of Children of Divorce: Marital Disruption and Parental Contact," *American Sociological Review*, vol. 48, no. 5.

Love is so much more than a feeling; rather, it's a decision we need to make every day to love our spouses and our children regardless of how we feel. We have reduced love to a mere feeling, and we are letting our feelings be our guide, and that can be a dangerous mistake since our feelings are capricious and influenced by many different factors.

My mom, in her wisdom, used to say that marriage is all about sacrifice. If we don't learn to die to ourselves so we can live for our spouses and our children, marriages and families could never survive. I'm seeing my mom's wisdom played out in our modern society as we watch the people we love suffering from the devastating trauma of divorce. Are we forgetting that marriage is about sacrifice? I believe we are.

The Children Are the Victims

While we know that the couple involved in divorce will go through great pain and sorrow, it's the children who will unfortunately pay the ultimate price and be forever scarred with deep wounds that need healing.

The evil one loves to use those wounds to plant all kinds of lies in the children of divorce. Those lies are very much like the ones planted in my heart and soul after the abuse I suffered. And these lies, as I mentioned before, follow you right into your adult life, continuing to cause havoc in your life if not dealt with in the proper way. Adults whose parents divorced when they were children often say they are unhappy, insecure, lonely, and experience persistent anxiety.

As people of faith, we must rebuke the devil's lies and unite to help families who are at risk of divorce. We must understand the trauma divorce will cause the children involved and encourage couples to remain together if at all possible.

If you, or someone you know, is going through a tough time in your marriage, I urge you to look for help. Talk to your pastor, a counselor, or a family member. Family is the living home in which humanity is nurtured. The individual family cannot survive and it will disintegrate unless it is kept safe within the larger family of the Church. Let's all unite in love and with compassion while at the same time bringing up the very important fact that the kids will indeed suffer greatly from divorce and will be at a very high risk of not being "just fine," as the devil would like us to believe.

One of the ways the devil tries to tear down society and the Church is through the destruction of the family. We need to ask God for the courage to fight and do whatever it takes to save our families from the destruction of divorce. We have to remember and remind those couples that all marriages go through ups and downs, and that is a normal thing.

Every day, let all of us who are married strive to do something for our spouses that we don't feel like doing; that way, we can get better at choosing to love our spouses, even during those times when we don't feel like loving him or her. With the grace of God and looking for the right help when we see that our marriages are in trouble, we can save our children from the terrible trauma that divorce will bring on them.

Let us also pray and support those who have gone through the trauma of divorce. And together we can be a beacon of light and healing for anyone who is hurting from this trauma.

CONCLUSION

For someone like me (and maybe you) who grew up thinking I was too broken to ever amount to anything or that God would never use me for anything purposeful, I would like to mention a few ways he's using me in hopes that you understand that no matter what lies you have been listening to, God does want to use us. All he needs is our yes!

A little over four years ago, I felt called (while at daily Mass) to start a women's apostolate. Our mission statement is simple: "To inspire mothers and daughters and women in general, through the guidance of the Holy Spirit, with inspirational talks and practical ways to live our beautiful Catholic faith in our everyday lives." Through this apostolate, that culminates with a mother/daughter spiritual brunch every year in May, one of our goals is to show other women what authentic sisterhood looks like. It's women helping women be what God created them to be: beloved daughters of the King.

I believe that this kind of sisterhood is a very important part of salvation history. As women of faith, who are striving for heaven, now more than in any other time in history we need to stick together and help each other navigate this crazy world we live in. The world is in desperate need of our witness to this sisterhood.

With the help of a few but very dedicated women who include my dear friends Sara Aiello and Kara Martinez as my core planning team, and many more who help in the background, we are about to celebrate our fourth annual spiritual brunch.

As Fr. Putnam stated so well when he came to bless our last event, more than ever we the faithful need to live in community, and this apostolate and brunch is a great example of that. We host upwards of two hundred mothers and daughters at these events who are eager to come and enjoy special time together, while at the same time also grow in the knowledge and appreciation of our rich Catholic faith. My prayer is that through this apostolate, women's hearts will be converted, much like how mine was converted at those young adults and coffee gatherings back in Bismarck.

The outpouring of love and support that we have received from women in our parish and beyond is what keeps us excited and looking forward to continuing this tradition for years to come. I hope to see these events take off in parishes throughout our country. I would gladly mentor any woman who feels called to start one in her community.

When I felt called to start this apostolate, I also heard God tell me that this was only the beginning and more would come after my yes. In the middle of a sleepless night in the fall of 2018, I got the inspiration to write my first book, titled *Wisdom from the Women We Love*. In this book, I joined twenty-four other women of different ages and backgrounds to share short stories of faith, hope, and love. When I first got the inspiration, I felt the Lord was telling me that this book would serve to help women everywhere know that they are never alone in their struggles.

The book is also supposed to help open women's eyes to all the beautiful teachings of our Church in a storytelling format, much like what Jesus did with parables. Each story has an accompanying Scripture verse, as well as questions to promote reflection for individual readers and book club participants.

I see that book as an extension of the women's apostolate and a great reminder that when we make time for God, he will do amazing things in us and through us. With the success of the first edition, I can foresee a second one in the future.

And clearly, this book is also part of God's plan on how he wants to use me. I believe that if we can assist God in healing our women, we who were created to be healers, we can then help him heal our men and our children. Call me naive, but I do believe that's possible. We must find healing ourselves first if we want to be used by God in helping others heal.

I do not know how you came to have and read this book. Perhaps a friend gave it to you. Perhaps you picked it up in the back of a church.

But however it came to you, I pray it has helped you in some way. I pray that you will, like me, find healing through charity, through forgiveness, through trust, and through the treasures Jesus has given us in his Church. Even if my words only prompt you to take that first step toward healing and coming out of the darkness, it was all worth it. The Holy Spirit will guide you the rest of the way.

I want to leave you with just a few parting comments.

First of all, God loves you. You are precious in his eyes and he wants to use you. He longs to heal you and mold you back into a beautiful piece of artwork. Statistically speaking, you or I aren't supposed to amount to much. Statistically speaking, we are supposed to succumb to a life of self-destruction through drugs, alcohol, depression, and mental illness. But thankfully, we have a God who doesn't look at statistics. He looks at our hearts and sees his child.

There's only one problem: he can't do this if you still believe in the evil one's lies. Those lies are like chains keeping you from moving toward God. You have to know that healing is possible. You can and you will find peace. To some, that may sound obvious, but I know from personal experience that when you are going through such pain, there doesn't seem to be any hope. Hang on to that hope. I am living proof that healing is possible. I was in as dark as place as anyone, and now I live in the light of Jesus.

One thing we have to remember, though, is that God will not force himself on anyone. He desires that we all come to him out of our own free will and give him our brokenness and pain. I realize now that for many years I didn't allow God to come into my deepest wound, and that was a big mistake. If you find that you are making that same mistake, I beg you to please stop! I wish I had a book like this in my twenties when I was going through my own dark valley. Let him in. That's how the healing begins.

Throughout the last few years, God has been extremely good to me in so many different ways. One was that my suffering was not in vain. Yours isn't either. Suffering never is. I can say from experience that all our amazing saints were right when, in their writings, they talk over and over about the value of suffering. I love how St. Paul of the Cross boldly expressed, "The Cross is the way to Paradise, but only when it's borne willingly."

I have willingly discerned to let God use me and my life story as a way to ease someone else's sufferings and help them see that they are not alone. We also need to understand that without the cross, we can't possibly have the Resurrection. I praise and glorify the Lord for allowing me to suffer because I'm afraid that without it, my faith would not be as strong as it is today. My brokenness brought me to him. So yes, now I can finally say that I am thankful for my scars. Would I be taking the time to know and trust in the Lord had it not been for my childhood trauma, and consequently my healing through Christ? Maybe, but I cannot say for sure. It is a mysterious thing, but I feel closer to Jesus in my sufferings.

Like the saints knew so well, God has a purpose for our suffering. If we learn to accept and embrace our crosses, and most importantly unite our sufferings with Christ's sufferings by offering them up for others, we would live a much more joy-filled life.

We also need to stop believing in what our modern secular society is trying to instill in us, that we shouldn't suffer or, even worse, that if there was a God, he wouldn't allow us to suffer. Those are terrible lies that the evil one loves to spread, and we need to be aware of them and pray to God that we don't fall for those lies. It is precisely because God loves us so much and knows us so well that he allows suffering to occur. He knows it can purify us and get us to heaven.

If Jesus, who is all perfect and all holy, had to suffer and die an awful death for my sins, what makes me think that I, who was already born a sinner, will not suffer? God tells us that we will have tribulations in this life. Happiness requires suffering. When we make the decision to accept our physical, emotional, and spiritual trials, then and only then we will find true happiness and become a saint.

One of my favorite saints, Pope St. John Paul II, who knew suffering firsthand and from a very young age, had this to say about suffering, "It is suffering, more than anything else, which clears the way for the grace which transforms human souls. Suffering more than anything else makes present in the history of humanity the powers of the Redemption."[5] Sacred Scripture also reminds us, "Suffering produces endurance, and endurance produces character, and character produces hope, and hope does not disappoint us, because God's love has been poured into our hearts through the Holy Spirit who has been given to us" (Rom 5:3–5).

As I grow in my faith, I'm learning that it's how you handle your sufferings, and how you let God be glorified through those trials, that makes all the difference in your happiness. I pray that all my past and future sufferings, and yours, will become for us a source of sanctification and an instrument of our salvation, and that we, like the saints who have gone before us, can be examples to a world that works so hard to erase all suffering.

The healing of our body, mind, and spirit is a lifelong process, an unfolding of God's perfect plan for us as we learn

---

[5]   Pope St. John Paul II, apostolic letter *On the Christian Meaning of Human Suffering* (*Salvifici Doloris*).

to surrender ourselves to his healing love. Every day, I make a conscious choice to believe in God's wonderful promises rather than in the devil's lies. I pray that you'll learn to do the same in your life.

In closing, let me ask you a series of questions:

- Who do you need to forgive?
- Do you truly desire God's healing and freedom through Christ?
- Do you wish to break free from all those chains that have kept you a prisoner?
- Do you believe that God wants nothing more than to be your healer and comforter?
- Will you allow him?
- Are you ready to start saying yes to the Lord, trusting that he will provide for all that you need?
- Are you ready to start believing that broken people like you and I are exactly the people he wants to use to accomplish his will and heal others?

Ask yourself these questions over the next few days. The answers might just change your life.

Here is a prayer I would like to close with that I wrote and now pray every day. Please feel free to use it or change it any way you like to make it your own:

Dear Jesus, I ask with all my heart that you remove anything and everything in me that's getting in the way of you accomplishing the work you started in me. Prune me and make me to better please you. I know that I'm nothing without you, Lord. My deepest desire is to know

and love you more and more every day. Please do not refuse me this favor and be with me today. Amen

HEALING TRAUMA IN THE BODY, MIND, AND SPIRIT

"Whoever wishes to heal man must see him in his wholeness and must know that his ultimate healing can only be God's love."

—Pope Benedict XVI, *Jesus of Nazareth*

Caring for the Soul as well as the Mind and Body

When I first began working as a pastoral counselor and psychotherapist, I never imagined myself specializing in trauma. In that stage of my career, I found that clients came to my office for something else: anxiety over a life-transition, struggles in an intimate relationship, unexplained panic or episodes of depression, and more.

But as the counseling relationship deepened in safety, trust, and care, clients felt more comfortable to go to the core of the wound, and many began to recall memories of childhood trauma. To meet the needs of my clients who struggled to trust others with their experience, I attended various trauma trainings in search of ways to help them heal.

When I found myself working with complex trauma, or those with particularly traumatizing childhoods and layered traumatic experiences, I very often left intensive trauma seminars disappointed and in search of more.

Although psychology can tell us a lot of valuable information about how the brain and traumatized body responds and ways of integrating traumatic memories into experience, I left these trainings wanting more because, in a sense, they were incomplete. While modern psychology teaches us invaluable information about the brain and the body, it fails to address *the care of the soul*. Ultimate healing must involve the healing of the whole person: body, mind, and soul.

Attachment theory shows us that a human being needs love in order to grow and thrive. Without love, we get sick in body, mind, and spirit. Love is the source of healing. While learning positive coping skills and ways of managing anxiety and depression is incredibly valuable, it does not lead to ultimate healing. There is no medication that provides a cure for PTSD, or anxiety or depression for that matter. To cure an illness, we must get to the source. Traumatic experiences create a series of wounds, but the method of healing is the same. The wounded part needs an encounter with Love. "Beloved, let us love one another; for love is of God, and he who loves is born of God and knows God. He who does not love does not know God; for God is love" (1 Jn 4:7–8).

All of us have traumas, times when we weren't treated with love. These traumas, whether large or small, create a wound. Traumas such as physical or sexual abuse create woundedness in the totality of a person. Just as a physical wound that remains open is prone to infection, a trauma wound creates an opening for lies to enter and infect the soul. An act of abuse carries with it a message of violence that poisons our experience; our very being is revolting against this experience of hatred. Deep down our body and soul knows this is not what we were created for. We were created out of love, for love.

We all have a story. We all have periods of triumph and tribulation, experiences of happiness and the pain of loss. Elza has given us a beautiful witness of healing from sexual abuse. However, we also know that each survivor's story is different. Healing takes time. We all have our unique walk with God. No matter what your walk has looked like, or where you are in your journey, your story matters. *You matter.* The Lord is yearning for you. He longs to heal you.

When a person avoids dealing with trauma, the effects begin to take over every aspect of their life. Trauma survivors often report feeling abandoned and alone, fearful and unable to trust others. Many report feeling hopeless that things could get better, and they feel powerless to make a change. They are confused about how they feel or why things happen, often feeling like it was their fault. This leads them to feel rejected, unlovable, bad, dirty, or damaged because of what happened to them.

Many mistakenly believe that all a trauma survivor needs to do is tell their story about what happened to them, and then they will be set free. Although telling our story is a very important part of healing (as we saw with Elza), it is not all of it. Current trauma research shows us that trauma memories are stored in our bodies. We don't have to dig into the past to see and feel the effects of trauma. For trauma survivors, the effects of trauma are likely showing up in daily life.

What Do Triggers Look Like?

Sudden, intense emotions, episodes of anxiety or fear, increased heart rate, tightness in the stomach, shallow breathing, hyperventilation or holding breath, obsessive thinking, overreacting to situations, muscle tension, twitches or tics, catastrophic, negative thinking, a sense of unbelonging, being on the outside looking in, feeling small, intense fear of abandonment or being alone.

Does this sound familiar? If you've had an experience where you felt that your life as you know it was threatened, then you likely know what it's like to experience a trigger.

Post-traumatic stress disorder is a condition resulting from exposure to a real or threatened serious injury or sexual assault. Studies have found that a serious traumatic event alters the brain and the ways we experience the world in our bodies and minds. Some symptoms of PTSD include:

1. Re-experiencing the traumatic event through disturbing thoughts, images, nightmares, distressing dreams, and flashbacks, and having intense negative emotions when reminded of the event.
2. Avoidance of anything that reminds one of the event.
3. Negative changes in thinking and mood, including inability to recall parts of the traumatic event, persistent negative beliefs and expectations about oneself, others, and the world, inappropriate blaming of oneself for the trauma, feeling spoiled or ruined by the trauma, and loss of interest in things one used to enjoy and feeling detached from others.
4. Feeling on edge, jumpy, reactive, irritable, struggling

with sleep or concentration, fearful of something happening again, self-harming or self-punishing, reckless actions.

If this sounds familiar, it's a good idea to seek professional help from someone experienced in treating PTSD. But to reinforce what was said earlier, seek one who is also open to treating the whole person (body, mind, and spirit).

What Does Healing Look Like?

First, we must make a decision to heal. This means acknowledging what has happened to us and saying "yes" to the healing that God has in mind for us. We are not meant to do this alone. The initial stages when one is dealing with repressed memories and things are beginning to resurface can be frightening. We must learn to trust the wisdom of our bodies and the Spirit that lives within us. Our bodies don't allow these things to resurface until we are ready. There's no need to go digging for memories, but when things begin to come up, it means that it's time to deal with it.

This is when it may be time to tell the Lord and another trusted person about what has happened. Saying these things aloud helps to dispel the shame that comes with the trauma. When we go through this process with a trained professional, the negative beliefs about ourselves or the lies are exposed. This involves accepting what happened and understanding that what happened wasn't your fault. Survivors often begin to realize that the things they believed about themselves for so long that may have affected the way they related to themselves and others are not true. This also involves grieving the loss of innocence if the abuse happened in childhood.

Another important aspect of healing is getting in touch with the body. Many trauma survivors are disconnected from their bodies since their bodies have become a source of shame. Dealing with triggers as they are being experienced in the body in the present moment is a way of integrating the trauma. A counselor who specializes in PTSD can also help you to understand your body's response to the trauma and help you to release the trauma from the body.

A survivor must also look at how they responded to the trauma. Many times, this involves understanding and self-forgiveness. Often survivors of sexual abuse sexually act out in some way, either through masturbation or reenacting the themes of the abuse with others. This can also look like becoming sexually promiscuous as a way to gain control over the abuse. These sexual actions are often a source of deep shame, and the shame is often compounded by a shallow understanding of the Church's teaching on sexuality. Such confusion may deepen the survivor's feelings of being unloved or unacceptable to God. Healing in this area involves developing a healthy relationship with the body and establishing healthy boundaries. Often a survivor must confront deep anger at the abuser, themselves, and others for how they may have responded, in addition to anger at God for "allowing" this to happen. Healing from this part involves forgiveness, which goes beyond acceptance to experiencing compassion for self and others. At this point and throughout the healing process, it is important to ask the Lord for healing, bringing our brokenness and vulnerability to him in trust and surrender.

What to Do if You're in Crisis

If you want to heal, if you make that conscious decision, but are feeling overwhelmed, try journaling. Journaling is a wonderful way to release your feelings and begin to gather your thoughts. You can also develop positive coping skills or ways to self-soothe, such as taking a warm bath, having a warm cup of tea, listening to relaxing music, drawing, or even cleaning.

This may sound obvious, but don't forget to breathe. Taking ten deep breaths can activate the parasympathetic nervous system; it's like hitting the reset button. Eat wholesome foods and exercise. Learning to nourish your body is an important step on the road to healing.

Develop a support system. Call a friend. Do something you enjoy. We all need people to lean on. Learn to ask for help. Give back; volunteer work is a great way to take your mind off what you're going through and find joy in helping others. Create a safe place inside. This could be a safe place inside your home, or also a safe place inside your mind.

Don't Be Afraid to Ask for Help

The wound of trauma happens in relationship to others, and the healing also must happen in relationship. For many trauma survivors, a skilled therapist or counselor is an integral part of the healing process. A good counselor is like a guide through the desert, someone who is familiar with the terrain and can offer support, encouragement, compassion, and insight. A counselor may be the first person to hear the whole story. This person can provide a safe place or "container" for the pain. I've had a survivor share that they never fully understood the horror they had endured or felt compassion for themselves until they saw it on my face. There was something about saying it aloud to another person that made the pain real, and I felt safe to connect with that part of myself, that part that had been locked away.

All trauma survivors are in need of an experience of God's mercy. Jesus shows us how mercy is the proper response to those in suffering. Mercy is a heart that yearns to give itself to another who is suffering and in turn is nourished by it. Mercy is a gift from God. Pope St. John Paul II, in his encyclical letter *The Mercy of God*, talks about how mercy brings about justice. "Mercy that is truly Christian is also the most perfect incarnation of 'equality' between people. . . . Mercy brings it about that people meet one another in that value which is [the dignity of each person]." In the counseling room, the mercy shown by the counselor brings about justice. Thus, human dignity is restored in relationship with the counselor who is also part of the Body of Christ.

I'm embarrassed to admit that it took me years of searching to fully grasp that the true healing of the whole person is found most completely in Jesus Christ. The true work of Christianity is the work of healing and deliverance: freedom from the things that bind us and prevent us from living the lives we were created to live as the people we were created to be. I've witnessed many who struggle with issues of forgiveness, struggling to forgive their abuser but also themselves. Perhaps there were those who did nothing to protect or stop the abuse from happening whom also need forgiveness. One survivor shared her own struggles with feeling abandoned. In time, the Lord revealed that he was not only present during her suffering but suffering with her.

How we understand suffering also impacts our relationship with God. A woman who had battled depression for years describes her belief that she was suffering as punishment for the sins of her past. She was believing a lie that was preventing her from receiving God's love. She didn't understand that God didn't desire to punish her but to love her.

So, if God isn't punishing me, then why didn't he save me from the parent who beat me or the person who abused me? Think about Jesus, the Father's only Son, whom he loved more than anything. Why didn't he remove his suffering? Because suffering is the means by which healing is obtained. Suffering is an experience of evil. Not all suffering is redemptive. It is our response to the suffering that determines whether it becomes a source of healing for others. When we take our suffering and offer it to God, we not only receive healing for ourselves but we can also become agents of healing for others.

How can our redemptive suffering become a source of healing for others? I remember sitting across from a woman who had been wrestling with forgiving her perpetrator. She was recalling how in a dream she felt the intense desire to pray for her perpetrator and had been doing so daily. She received the call and said yes. Through the process of praying for her perpetrator, she was able to forgive and experienced immense healing and peace.

I've experienced firsthand that our calling is on the other side of woundedness. The Lord works all things for good for those who love him. When we offer our whole selves to God, he takes our wounds and creates something beautiful. The Lord brings meaning to the suffering by giving it purpose and significance in helping others.

The Lord wants us to come as we are. Don't be afraid to bring your wounds to God. Don't be afraid to ask for help. You are loved. You are enough and you are not alone.

The Peace Prayer of St. Francis of Assisi

Make me a channel of your peace,
Where there is hatred let me bring your love,
Where there is injury your pardon Lord,
And where there's doubt true faith in you.

Make me a channel of your peace,
Where there's despair in life, let me bring hope,
Where there is darkness, only light,
And where there's sadness, ever joy.

O Master grant that I may never seek,
So much to be consoled as to console,
To be understood as to understand,
To be loved as to love with all my soul.

Make me a channel of your peace,
It is in pardoning that we are pardoned,
In giving of ourselves that we receive.
And in dying that we're born to eternal life.

Christine Wisdom, M.S. LPC
Pastoral Counselor and Psychotherapist in Huntersville, NC

Note: This section was written from the counselor's personal experience for a Christian/Catholic audience. Those who are not Christian or Catholic may not relate to the themes or method of healing presented here. This is not meant to represent the opinions or positions of all Licensed Professional Counselors or other mental health professionals.

ACKNOWLEDGMENTS

A special thanks to my beloved pastor Father John Putnam for having the wisdom of knowing what I needed that day in confession and for walking that road with me, and for being my mentor and sounding board. I know that this book would not exist if not for you being there for me through and through. It would have been too difficult to write about this difficult topic without your constant, fatherly support. I'm so glad God chose you to be the vessel he would use to heal me, and I'm forever grateful for that. We are truly blessed to have someone like you as our leader at St. Mark. May God continue to bless, protect, guide, and give you all that you need to persevere in your priestly calling with the same love and zeal as always. Please be assured of my unending prayers!

To Father Paul McNulty, who also walked the road to healing with me and for giving so much of his precious time to encourage and be there for me when I needed someone. You are also in my daily prayers and I'm forever grateful for your kindness and compassion and for your special gift of healing! You are such a blessing to all of us! Thank you for answering the call to the priesthood!

A special thanks to Neal Lozano, the author of *Unbound*, for having the courage to write such a profound and much needed book that has helped millions of us understand how to free ourselves from the chains that the evil one attaches to us through the many different types of trauma. And for being so kind and gracious with his time by answering my emails and even calling me on the phone to encourage me to write my story. His compassion and support in the beginnings of this project are deeply appreciated.

To Christine Wisdom for graciously agreeing to write the epilogue for the book and for being the first counselor I have ever encountered who acknowledged that healing can and will only come through our Lord Jesus Christ.

To my friend Catherine Farley, who's a very accomplished writer and guided me in the direction of TAN Books by providing me with the right contact. You have been a blessing in so many ways.

To my new friend Michelle Bell for bringing my vision of the cover to life. You nailed it! You are such an incredibly talented artist, and I know God will continue doing amazing things in you and through you. You are his beloved daughter!

A big thanks to Brian Kennelly at Saint Benedict Press and TAN Books for believing that my story could make an impact, and for helping this newbie understand the book and the publishing business by answering the endless questions I had. Thank you for your patience, guidance, and kindness. And thank you for making the book better by doing the necessary editing.

To my loving husband for always being my rock and for giving me the support I needed to get through with this difficult project. I love you so much and I'm so thankful that God has gifted me such a great man for a husband. You and the kids are my most precious gifts from God and words cannot express how much I love each of you.

To my dear friend Jennifer Creter, who helped me realize that I had never talked about the painful details of what was actually done to me. She offered to come over to my house while the kids were at school to type those difficult details as I sat and told her everything. The love and compassion you showed me is something I will never forget. Please know that I'm always here for you.

To my friend Brian Keenan, who shares my love for reading and happily said yes to my request of going through the manuscript looking for any area or subject that I needed to go deeper. You made some great recommendations and I took them all into consideration.